MARTIAL ARTS
SPORTS ZONE

AMATEUR WRESTLING

COMBAT ON THE MAT

Garrison Wells

Lerner Publications Company • Minneapolis

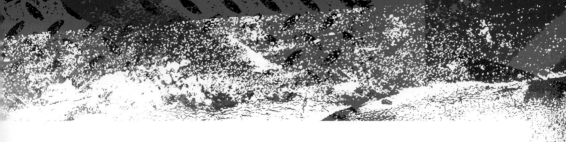

Lerner Publications Company
A division of Lerner Publishing Group, Inc.
241 First Avenue North
Minneapolis, MN 55401 U.S.A.

Website address: www.lernerbooks.com

Content Consultant: Jim Andrassy, Head Wrestling Coach, Kent State University, Kent, Ohio

Library of Congress Cataloging-in-Publication Data

Wells, Garrison.
    Amateur wrestling : combat on the mat / by Garrison Wells.
        p.   cm.
    Includes index.
    ISBN 978–0–7613–8460–1 (lib. bdg. : alk. paper)
    1. Wrestling—Juvenile literature. I. Title.
  GV1195.3.W68 2012
  796.812—dc23   2011033395

Manufactured in the United States of America
1 – BC – 12/31/11

Photo Credits: Ed Wray/AP Images, 5; Nicholas Piccillo/Shutterstock Images, 6, 17 (bottom), 18; Mikhail Metzel/AP Images, 7; Rob Stapleton/AP Images, 8; Trevor Brown/AP Images, 9; Archive Photos/Getty Images, 11; Popperfoto/Getty Images, 13; Mark J. Terrill/AP Images, 14; iStockphoto, 17 (top); Aaron Ontiveroz/AP Images, 19; Joe Connell/AP Images, 21; 123RF, 23; Susan Leggett/Bigstock, 24; Iurii Konoval/Shutterstock Images, 25; Charlie Neibergall/AP Images, 26; Walter Hinick/AP Images, 28 (bottom); Dave Peterson/AP Images, 28 (top); Cameron Spencer/Getty Images, 29
Backgrounds: Aleksandar Velasevic/iStockphoto, iStockphoto, Nicholas Piccillo/Shutterstock Images
Cover: AP Photo/Carolyn Kaster (main); © iStockphoto.com/Aleksandar Velasevic (background)
Main body text set in ITC Serif Gothic Std Bold 11/17.
Typeface provided by Adobe Systems.

TABLE OF CONTENTS

CHAPTER ONE

AMATEUR WRESTLING

Henry Cejudo dreamed of someday winning an Olympic title. He was a state wrestling champion as a high school freshman and sophomore. Then he moved to Colorado at the age of 16 to train at the U.S. Olympic Training Center.

It was a unique path to take. Most U.S. Olympic wrestlers compete for a college team before wearing the red, white, and blue. Cejudo was an exception. At the age of 21, Cejudo qualified for the Olympic Games. He competed in the freestyle division. In the gold medal match, he defeated Japan's Tomihiro Matsunaga. That made Cejudo the youngest U.S. wrestler to win an Olympic gold medal. He had achieved his dream of becoming an Olympic champion.

AMATEUR WRESTLING DEFINED

Amateur wrestling is a contest in which two opponents face each other on a mat. They fight using their bodies to win points or to pin their opponents to the mat. (A pin is a hold that a wrestler cannot get out of.)

Henry Cejudo (*right*) won a gold medal in freestyle wrestling at the 2008 Olympic Games.

"Once you've wrestled, everything in life is easy."

—Dan Gable, U.S. amateur wrestler, gold medal winner in the 1972 Olympic Games

Amateur wrestlers are not paid to compete. Amateur wrestling is well known as an Olympic sport. It is also practiced in schools and colleges across the United States.

TYPES OF AMATEUR WRESTLING

There are three main types of amateur wrestling. The first is folkstyle. It is mostly practiced in the United States. Folkstyle focuses on wrestling on the mat. All high school and college wrestling is folkstyle wrestling.

The second is Greco-Roman. This form is practiced standing up, and it stresses throws. Wrestlers are not allowed to use their legs or hold their opponents below the waists. This type of wrestling is practiced around the world.

The third is freestyle. Freestyle is a combination of Greco-Roman and folkstyle. It is mostly stand-up wrestling. But it has short bursts of fighting on the mat.

Folkstyle wrestling is a popular sport in high schools across the United States.

Greco-Roman and freestyle are the most common wrestling styles worldwide. Greco-Roman and freestyle are the only wrestling categories in the Olympic Games. These two styles are also taught to kids and young adults in wrestling clubs.

Freestyle and folkstyle are the most common types of wrestling in the United States. A mixed form of wrestling called grappling has grown in popularity too. Grappling combines many different martial arts forms. These include Brazilian jiujitsu, sambo, judo, freestyle wrestling, folkstyle wrestling, and Greco-Roman wrestling.

COMPETITION

Wrestling competitions are called matches. Wrestlers are divided into age and weight divisions to make sure matches are fair. This is mostly because heavier opponents have an advantage due to their size and natural strength. Winners are determined in each weight and age class.

There are many throws in Greco-Roman wrestling, which does not require headgear.

WRESTLING AGE DIVISIONS

USA WRESTLING IS THE OFFICIAL NATIONAL GOVERNING BODY OF WRESTLING IN THE UNITED STATES. THE ORGANIZATION SETS UP GROUPS OF FREESTYLE, FOLKSTYLE, AND GRECO-ROMAN WRESTLERS FROM EIGHT-YEAR-OLDS TO OLYMPIANS. BOYS AND MEN HAVE 10 DIVISIONS. GIRLS AND WOMEN HAVE 9. OLYMPIANS COMPETE IN THE SENIOR DIVISION.

High school wrestling during a tournament

Each individual wrestling competition has three periods. Every level of wrestling has a different length of time for each period. Each period is two minutes long in high school. In college, the first period is three minutes. The last two periods are two minutes.

School teams are pitted against one another in school competitions. There are several types of competitions. A dual meet is when one school competes against one other school. A round-robin tournament is for more than two schools. A regular bracket tournament is usually for six or more schools. The team that scores the most points wins the tournament.

SCORING

Wrestlers earn points by doing successful techniques. Points are different in freestyle and Greco-Roman wrestling. In folkstyle, a takedown is worth two points. This is any move that brings an

A college wrestler tries to get his opponent to the mat.

ILLEGAL MOVES IN AMATEUR WRESTLING

- STRIKING WITH HANDS, ELBOWS, FEET, KNEES, OR THE HEAD
- PAINFULLY BENDING JOINTS AND FINGERS
- CHOKING, STRANGLING, AND SUFFOCATING
- SLAMMING YOUR OPPONENT HEADFIRST ONTO THE MAT
- GRABBING YOUR OPPONENT'S GENITALS
- HOLDING YOUR OPPONENT'S UNIFORM

opponent to the mat. An escape is worth one point. In this move, a wrestler gets out from under the opponent. A reversal is worth two points. This is when the wrestler is first under the opponent and then shifts to be on top. Back points are points awarded for putting an opponent's back within 90 degrees of the mat. The wrestler with the most points at the end of a match wins. The other way to win is by pinning an opponent.

In Greco-Roman and freestyle wrestling, a wrestler can also win with a technical fall. This happens by scoring a certain number of points or performing certain techniques in a period. If a wrestler wins two of the three periods of a match by technical fall, he or she wins the match.

CHAPTER TWO
HISTORY AND CULTURE

Amateur wrestling is one of the oldest styles of fighting. It has been around for thousands of years. Proof of its history has been found in China, Egypt, India, France, and other countries. Archaeologists in Egypt have found art dating back to 2300 B.C. that shows wrestling. Drawings on cave walls in France show wrestling existed more than 15,000 years ago.

Modern amateur wrestling is mostly for sport. But in ancient times, it was used in battle as unarmed fighting. Greek and Roman soldiers practiced wrestling as part of their training. Greek women, who were called the Spartan girls, also wrestled. They were not soldiers. But they wrestled as a way to keep in shape and compete.

Amateur wrestling was soon turned into a sport with a scoring system. It had rules for safety too. Wrestling became part of the ancient Greek Olympics in 708 B.C. Other ancient people also used wrestling as a martial art. These groups included the early Chinese, early Europeans, and the ancient Egyptians. Europeans first came to

Ancient Greeks believed their gods took part in wrestling.

the Americas during the late 1400s. Wrestling was already established when they arrived. Native Americans practiced it for sport and self-defense.

AN OLYMPIC SPORT

Modern amateur wrestling began taking shape during the late 1800s. That is when the current wrestling styles were developed. Greco-Roman wrestling was the first style to gain popularity. It was designed to be like the ancient wrestling style.

In 1896 the first modern Olympic Games were held in Paris, France. Greco-Roman wrestling was one of nine sports included in those Games. Freestyle wrestling became an Olympic sport at the 1904 Games in Saint Louis, Missouri.

Beginning with the 1908 Games, the competitions were split into four weight classes for Greco-Roman and five weight classes for freestyle. However, some weight classes have been changed since then.

The rules of amateur wrestling became more defined in the decades that followed. One important rule was adding a time limit to matches. Another was adding a points system. College wrestling teams first created points in 1928 to determine a winner if neither wrestler was pinned.

Another important milestone was the formation of the International Amateur Wrestling Federation (FILA) during the early 1900s. The organization governs amateur wrestling around the world. FILA's most well-known role is organizing the Olympic wrestling tournament. It also has overseen the world championships for Greco-Roman and freestyle wrestling since the 1950s.

Wrestlers competed at the 1912 Olympic Games in Stockholm, Sweden.

Rulon Gardner won a bronze medal at the 2004 Olympics Games. After his final match, he left his shoes in the ring to show his retirement from the sport.

Only the Olympic Games are a bigger competition. However, FILA also sets up the rules and international competition for other levels of wrestling.

EMOTIONAL WIN

Wrestling remains one of the most anticipated events at the Olympic Games. It is also one of the most emotional events. Wrestling is a very grueling sport. The athletes at every level must put in tremendous work to be successful. That is most true at the Olympic level.

Rulon Gardner was a top U.S. Greco-Roman wrestler. At the 2000 Olympic Games in Sydney, Australia, he defeated Alexander Karelin of Russia

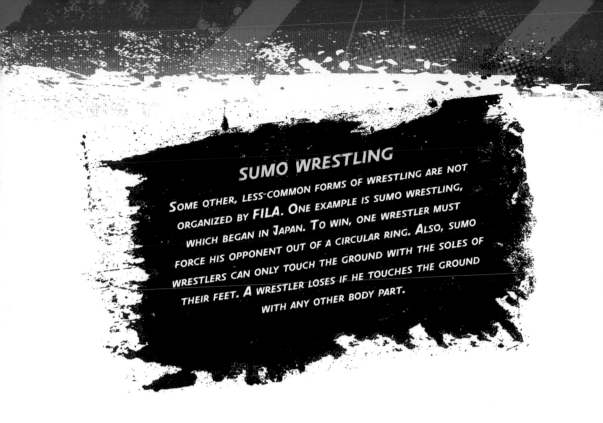

SUMO WRESTLING

Some other, less-common forms of wrestling are not organized by FILA. One example is sumo wrestling, which began in Japan. To win, one wrestler must force his opponent out of a circular ring. Also, sumo wrestlers can only touch the ground with the soles of their feet. A wrestler loses if he touches the ground with any other body part.

to win the gold medal. Many thought Karelin could not be beaten. He had not lost a match since 1987.

In 2004 Gardner overcame tremendous odds to return to the Olympic Games held in Athens, Greece. His comeback fell short of defending his gold medal. Gardner finished his career with a bronze in the super heavyweight division. Following the match, Gardner upheld a wrestling tradition. He removed his shoes and left them on the mat. "To leave them on the mat meant I left everything on the mat as a wrestler," Gardner said.

CHAPTER THREE

EQUIPMENT AND TECHNIQUES

The equipment used in amateur wrestling includes mats, headgear, shoes, and singlets. A singlet is a tight-fitting uniform made of a lightweight material. The tight fit keeps a wrestler's opponent from grabbing the uniform. It also helps the referee get a clear view of wrestlers' bodies for scoring. Female wrestlers wear singlets that go higher up on the body.

The headgear protects the ears and prevents head injuries. Made of plastic-covered foam, the headgear covers the ears like a pair of earmuffs. A strap underneath the chin holds the headgear in place. Headgear is required in high school and college wrestling in the United States. It is only allowed in the Olympic Games if approved by FILA. Headgear is optional in competitions in other countries.

The shoes that wrestlers wear are very light. They are ankle high for support. They give wrestlers traction on the mat. Padded foam mats protect wrestlers from injuries that can happen from takedowns, reversals, and other moves.

Wrestlers need to wear shoes that protect their ankles. Headgear protects the head and ears from injury.

COMMON TECHNIQUES

Techniques—such as takedowns, escapes, reversals, and pins—are important because a wrestler scores points when moves are done well. Techniques also put a wrestler in position to score more points or to win the match by getting a pin.

Everything starts with the takedown. The most common types are the single-leg and double-leg takedowns. The single-leg takedown is the most common. For this takedown, a wrestler snares an opponent's leg. Then the wrestler lifts the opponent's leg toward the chest. Then the wrestler drives through or turns the body to take the opponent to the mat. The double-leg takedown uses the same moves as the single leg, but both legs are grabbed.

Wrestlers begin a match in a low position so they can keep good balance.

A wrestler performs the single-leg takedown during a college match.

Most amateur wrestlers will tell you that their favorite technique is the pin. There's a simple reason for this. The pin leads to victory. It is the quickest way to end the match. To do a pin, a wrestler holds his or her opponent's shoulders to the mat for two seconds. The shoulder blades must be touching the mat.

A FORCE ON THE MAT

One wrestler known for his fast takedowns was Cael Sanderson. He dominated college wrestling like no man before him. Sanderson wrestled for four years at powerhouse Iowa State from 1998 to 2002. He went 159–0 during that time. Among his wins were four Division I championships. Division I college programs are able to offer athletic scholarships and are typically where the best athletes compete. One other college wrestler had won four titles. Only Sanderson did it while going undefeated.

AMATEUR TO PRO

Amateur wrestling can be a springboard to a career in professional wrestling or in mixed martial arts (MMA). Brock Lesnar won the National Collegiate Athletic Association (NCAA) heavyweight championship for the University of Minnesota in 2000. From there he moved to a successful career in the World Wrestling Entertainment (WWE). Next, he became a mixed martial artist. He won the Ultimate Fighting Championship heavyweight title in 2008.

Cael Sanderson *(left)* went undefeated during his four years of wrestling for Iowa State.

After college Sanderson set his sights on the 2004 Olympic Games. He lived up to expectations at the Games in Athens, Greece. Sanderson won the gold medal in the 84-kilogram (185-pound) freestyle division. Sanderson retired from wrestling soon after and became a college coach. He guided Penn State to the 2011 national title. Sanderson has since returned to the mat to qualify for the 2012 Olympic Games in London, England.

CHAPTER FOUR

MODERN WRESTLING

A mateur wrestling remains popular around the world. The sport often has a different name, but the techniques are similar. In China, for example, wrestling—called *shuai jiao*—is both a sport and a form of fighting. Some people believe it's the country's oldest martial art. Wrestling is known as *lucha libre* in Mexico and other Spanish-speaking countries. Lucha libre wrestlers wear masks. Amateur wrestling is also popular in Japan, Brazil, Australia, Bulgaria, Turkey, the Middle East, and other parts of the world.

OIL WRESTLING

ANOTHER FORM OF WRESTLING NOT OVERSEEN BY **FILA** IS OIL WRESTLING. THE WRESTLERS COMPETE WHILE COVERED IN OIL. OIL WRESTLING, OR GREASED WRESTLING, TAKES PLACE MOSTLY IN TURKEY. THE BIGGEST TOURNAMENT HAS BEEN HELD EVERY YEAR FOR MORE THAN **600** YEARS. A WRESTLER CAN WIN IN THREE WAYS. ONE IS IF HIS OPPONENT'S CHEST FACES THE SKY. ANOTHER IS IF THE WRESTLER LIFTS HIS OPPONENT ABOVE HIS SHOULDERS AND CARRIES HIM FOR THREE STEPS. THE THIRD WAY TO WIN IS BY PINNING THE OPPONENT.

Wrestlers compete in Turkey.

LEVELS OF WRESTLING

Amateur wrestling is practiced at almost all levels at many schools and wrestling clubs in the United States. Schools teach wrestling in gym classes. Schools also take part in competitions. The sport is a good way to exercise. Just a few minutes grappling on the mat can be a great workout. Wrestling also teaches students self-discipline. The sport helps build self-confidence too.

Competition in clubs can start at a very young age. Some kids start wrestling at five years old. The average age is probably around eight or nine.

Many wrestlers begin at a young age.

Competition in schools starts in middle school. At that level, a wrestler works on improving the basics, such as positioning, movement, and properly executing moves.

Wrestlers can move on to compete in high school. At this level, wrestlers learn more techniques. They represent their schools in bigger competitions. Top high school wrestlers can earn scholarships to college. At the college level, wrestlers are among the nation's best athletes. Top schools for college wrestling include Oklahoma State University, the University of Iowa, and the University of Minnesota. Many U.S. Olympic wrestlers first wrestled for a college team.

U.S. wrestlers have done well in the Olympic Games. Dan Gable was the first wrestler not to have a single point scored on him when he won a gold medal in 1972. Kurt Angle won gold in 1996. (He later became a professional wrestler.) Another famous U.S. Olympic wrestler is Bruce Baumgartner. He wrestled in the Olympic Games during the 1980s and the 1990s. He won four medals. This is the most a U.S. wrestler has won.

WOMEN AND WRESTLING

Women's wrestling was first added to the Olympic Games in 2004 in Athens, Greece. However, women wrestled long before that. Top U.S. female amateur wrestlers include Kristie Davis and Tricia Saunders. Davis won gold medals in 2000 and 2003 competing in women's world championships. USA Wrestling, the governing body for the sport in the United States, named Davis the Women's Wrestler of the Year in 2002. Saunders won four world championship gold medals, in 1992, 1996, 1998, and 1999.

Although most wrestlers are male, females still wrestle in high school and at higher levels.

A wrestler tries to pin his opponent.

Women only compete in freestyle wrestling at the Olympic Games. In 2008 18 medals were awarded in the women's division. Randi Miller of the United States won a bronze medal at the 2008 Games. She has become a mixed martial artist. Clarissa Chun, another U.S. wrestler, placed fifth.

HARD WORK PAYS OFF

Wrestling is a challenging sport. Performing well requires a lot of hard work and practice. The sport requires great physical fitness. Wrestlers need to be strong so they can overpower their opponents. They also need endurance. That is the ability to maintain a high level of physical effort for a long time.

Wrestling matches are decided by more than just physical fitness, though. The sport has a mental element. A wrestler has to be smart. That means knowing how to properly do moves. It also means knowing when to do certain moves. Having a sound strategy can be just as important as physical fitness. A wrestling match can be long and painful. Wrestlers need to be able to stay focused and to maintain a high level of performance even when tired or hurting.

Wrestling is unique from other sports in that competitors are matched against opponents of a similar size. Some wrestlers can be small and quick. Others might be large and powerful. What's great about wrestling is that people of different weights and sizes can compete. As long as they work hard and follow the rules, any wrestler can have success.

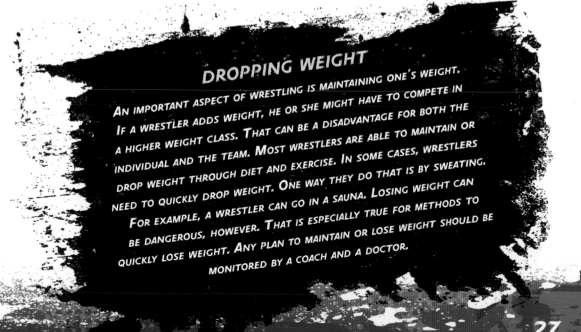

DROPPING WEIGHT

An important aspect of wrestling is maintaining one's weight. If a wrestler adds weight, he or she might have to compete in a higher weight class. That can be a disadvantage for both the individual and the team. Most wrestlers are able to maintain or drop weight through diet and exercise. In some cases, wrestlers need to quickly drop weight. One way they do that is by sweating. For example, a wrestler can go in a sauna. Losing weight can be dangerous, however. That is especially true for methods to quickly lose weight. Any plan to maintain or lose weight should be monitored by a coach and a doctor.

TOP WRESTLING MOVES

FIREMAN'S CARRY

In this move, a wrestler grabs the opponent's arm with one hand and pushes the other arm between the opponent's legs. Then the wrestler throws the opponent over the wrestler's shoulder. Because of the possibility of injury, the wrestler can only do this technique from the knees.

HALF NELSON

To do the half nelson, the opponent should be on the stomach. The wrestler gains control of the opponent's wrist, and then the wrestler pushes the other hand under the opponent's arm and behind the neck. The wrestler can then roll the opponent over onto his or her back for the pin.

GRAND AMPLITUDE THROW

AMPLITUDE REFERS TO THE HIGH, SWEEPING MOVE IN THIS TAKEDOWN. A WRESTLER GRABS THE OPPONENT LOW ON THE TORSO. THEN THE WRESTLER LIFTS THE OPPONENT UP AND FLIPS THE OPPONENT OVER, SO THE OPPONENT'S LEGS GO OVER THE HEAD.

TOP TEN
AMERICAN WRESTLERS

KURT ANGLE
This 1996 Olympic champion in freestyle went on to a successful professional wrestling career.

BRUCE BAUMGARTNER
He is the only U.S. wrestler to win four Olympic medals, including freestyle gold in 1984 and 1992.

HENRY CEJUDO
At age 21, this freestyle wrestler became the youngest U.S. wrestler to win a gold medal.

KRISTIE DAVIS
She won gold medals at the 2000 and 2003 world championships.

DAN GABLE
He became the Olympic freestyle champion in 1972.

RULON GARDNER
He defeated seemingly invincible Russian Alexander Karelin in Greco-Roman at the 2000 Olympic Games.

PATRICIA MIRANDA
She became the first female Olympic medal winner with a bronze in 2008.

CAEL SANDERSON
He is the only undefeated college wrestler. He also won an Olympic gold medal in freestyle in 2004.

TRICIA SAUNDERS
She was a four-time world champion gold medalist during the 1990s.

JOHN SMITH
He won Olympic gold medals in freestyle in 1988 and 1992.

GLOSSARY

AMPLITUDE

the high, sweeping range of motion in a popular takedown

ARCHAEOLOGIST

a person who studies ancient human life and activities

REFEREE

a person who judges or guides a sporting event

ROUND-ROBIN

describing a tournament where every team or player competes against each team or player in the tournament

SCHOLARSHIP

money that is given to students to help pay for school or living expenses as a reward for certain skills, such as academics or athletics

SENIOR DIVISION

the division for the oldest athletes wrestling in USA Wrestling events

SNARE

to capture and hold

TORSO

the midsection of the human body

TRACTION

power to grip the mat

FOR MORE INFORMATION

FURTHER READING

Chapman, Mike. *Wrestling Tough*. Champaign, IL: Human Kinetics, 2005.

Linde, Barbara M. *Olympic Wrestling*. New York: Rosen Publishing Group, 2007.

Page, Jason. *Martial Arts, Boxing, and Other Combat Sports*. New York: Crabtree Publishing, 2008.

Ryan, Thomas, and Julie Sampson. *Beginning Wrestling*. New York: Sterling Publishing, 2001.

WEBSITES

FILA
http://www.fila-wrestling.com
The official website of amateur wrestling's international governing body includes information about major competitions within the different styles of amateur wrestling.

InterMat
http://www.intermatwrestle.com
This website offers news about amateur wrestling, particularly at the high school and college levels.

USA Wrestling
http://www.themat.com
The official website of USA Wrestling includes news, event information, and other resources about all levels of amateur wrestling.

INDEX

ABOUT THE AUTHOR

Garrison Wells is a third-degree black belt in Nihon jujitsu, a first-degree black belt in judo, a third-degree black belt in Goju-ryu karate, and a first-degree black belt in kobudo. He is also an award-winning journalist and writer. Wells lives in Colorado.